Contents

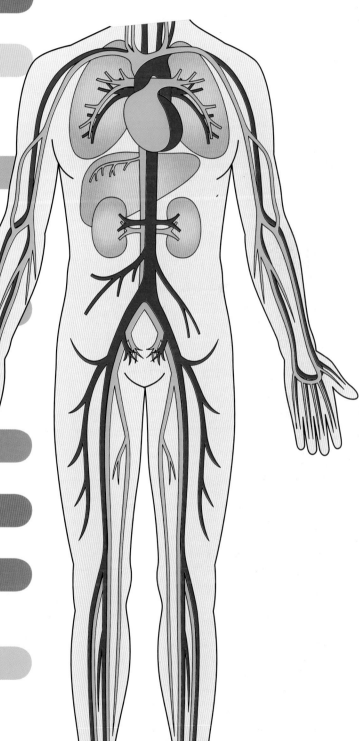

Introduction

The body has many tasks to perform. Here are some of the main tasks, and the parts of the body that do them.

Think of the body as the world's most amazing chemistry set in which chemical changes are going on all the time.

❶ The tiny building blocks that make up every part of our bodies are called **CELLS**. You can only see cells with a microscope. Our bodies are made up of more than 60 billion cells. Cells use food and **ENERGY** in the form of liquid chemicals. Find out about these remarkable building blocks on page 8.

❷ When we eat food or drink liquids, we are adding more

materials to our bodies which can be made into cells or used to keep us active. These materials are described on page 10.

❸ We break down our food into pieces small enough to swallow using our teeth. Find out why we have different kinds of teeth on page 12.

❹ Most foods contain a mixture of many materials, so one thing the body has to do is to break down (**DIGEST**) and then take in (**ABSORB**) the useful materials so that the cells can use them. How this happens is shown on page 14.

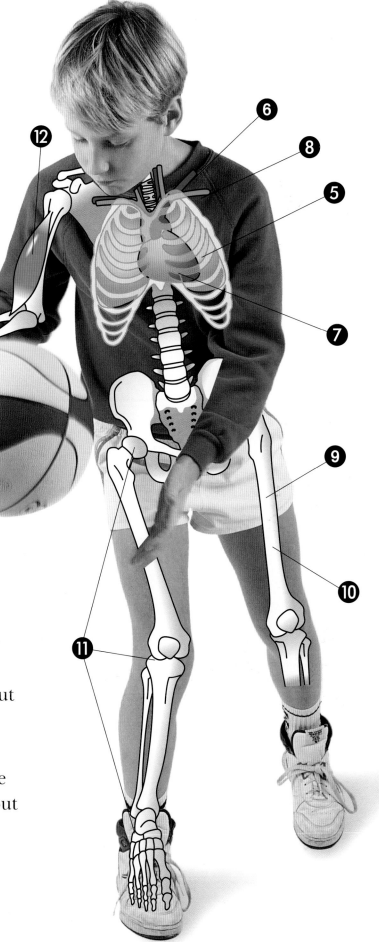

5 One of the most important ways of breaking down substances is to add oxygen. Oxygen and food together give out energy. Oxygen is taken in from the air by breathing. Find out how the lungs work on page 16.

6 The body is made up of lots of different cells. But cells continually need more supplies of food and energy. The best way of getting it to them is by bathing them in a liquid. The main liquid for doing this is called blood. Find out what blood does on page 18.

7 The heart is the pump that pushes the blood around. See how it works on page 20.

8 The movement of blood around the body is called circulation. Find out about **CIRCULATION** on page 22.

9 Our body has a shape because it is held up by our bones. Find out about bones on page 24.

10 Strangely, inside 'solid' bone is the place where new blood is made. The bones make up the skeleton. Find out about the skeleton on page 26.

11 Bones meet at joints. The body has many types of joints. See how they work on page 28.

5

12 The skeleton also acts as a support for the flesh – muscles and skin. See how muscles work on page 30. The skin is described on page 8.

13 Sometimes people describe bodies as marvellous computers. Computers are controlled by electricity, and so are we. All of the parts of our bodies are controlled by electrical signals from the brain. Electrical signals pass around our bodies through the **NERVES**, triggering the heart to pump, the legs to move and our brain to think. Find out about the brain and nerves on page 32.

14 Some of our cells can do more than make new versions of themselves. They can combine with cells from other bodies and make completely new people. This is called **REPRODUCTION**. Find out about this on page 34.

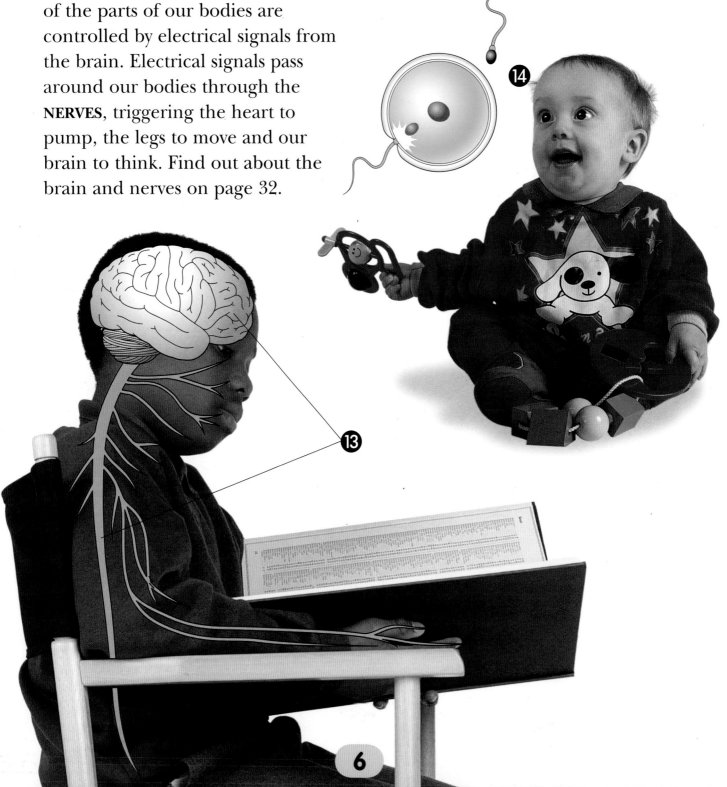

15 When we breathe, drink, eat or cut ourselves, we may accidentally take in small unpleasant **ORGANISMS**, which are often called **GERMS**. If the germs flourish, they multiply quickly and cause **DISEASES**. Find out about this on page 36.

16 The body has a special system for dealing with most diseases. This is called our **IMMUNE SYSTEM** and it is shown on page 38.

17 If we eat the wrong types or the wrong amounts of food, the body may not work properly. To stay healthy, we need to eat a balanced **DIET**. Find out how diet affects people on page 40.

18 Much of the body only works properly if it is exercised regularly. Find out why on page 42.

19 We can sometimes choose to override the body's defences. Doing this can cause permanent harm. Find out why on page 44.

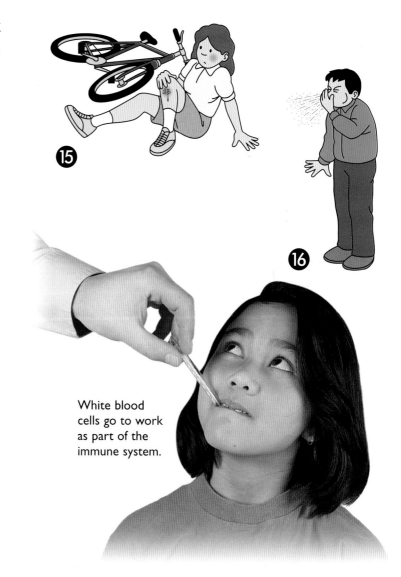

White blood cells go to work as part of the immune system.

7

Cells

Cells are the tiny building blocks of each body. They can form in many shapes and sizes. The body is made from billions of them.

If you want to know what a human body is made of, you have to look through a microscope.

When scientists first looked through a microscope at some living material, they were astonished to find that it was made up of tiny bags of jelly-like material, each with a little speck in the centre and surrounded by a rubbery bag (Pictures ① and ②). These bags are the cells which make up the body.

▼ ① **This is a cross section of a piece of skin. The large object sticking out is a hair. The skin shows clearly how the body makes many different kinds of cells, each suited to a special use.**

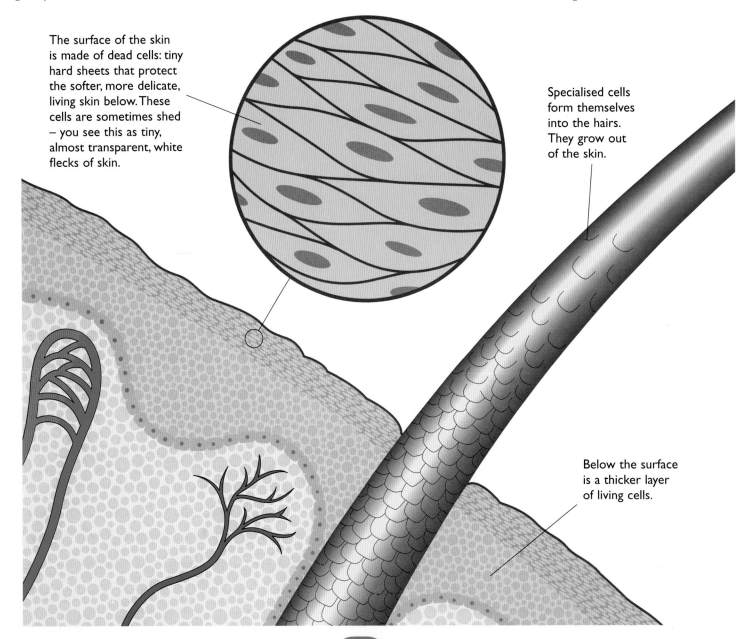

The surface of the skin is made of dead cells: tiny hard sheets that protect the softer, more delicate, living skin below. These cells are sometimes shed – you see this as tiny, almost transparent, white flecks of skin.

Specialised cells form themselves into the hairs. They grow out of the skin.

Below the surface is a thicker layer of living cells.

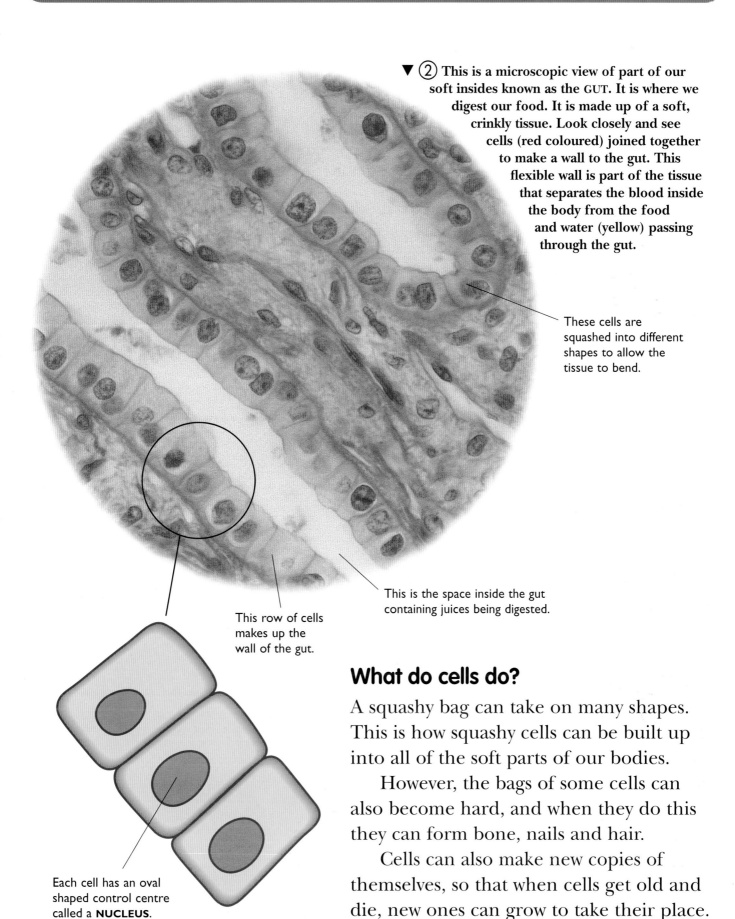

▼ ② This is a microscopic view of part of our soft insides known as the GUT. It is where we digest our food. It is made up of a soft, crinkly tissue. Look closely and see cells (red coloured) joined together to make a wall to the gut. This flexible wall is part of the tissue that separates the blood inside the body from the food and water (yellow) passing through the gut.

These cells are squashed into different shapes to allow the tissue to bend.

This is the space inside the gut containing juices being digested.

This row of cells makes up the wall of the gut.

Each cell has an oval shaped control centre called a **NUCLEUS**.

What do cells do?

A squashy bag can take on many shapes. This is how squashy cells can be built up into all of the soft parts of our bodies.

However, the bags of some cells can also become hard, and when they do this they can form bone, nails and hair.

Cells can also make new copies of themselves, so that when cells get old and die, new ones can grow to take their place.

Weblink: www.CurriculumVisions.com/body

Food

Food provides the energy and NOURISHMENT for living. Each food contains its own unique combination of nourishment and energy.

There are many kinds of food and drink, but every one is made of some, or all, of five groups of nutrients (Picture ①). They are called **CARBOHYDRATES** (sugar and **STARCH**), **FATS**, **PROTEINS**, **VITAMINS** (Picture ②) and **MINERALS** (Picture ③).

Carbohydrates and fats give energy. Proteins, vitamins and

minerals build new cells. Because each type of food does a different job, the body needs food containing each group – you cannot just eat one type of food and stay healthy.

Sugars and starches

Natural sugars are made of small particles that **DISSOLVE** in water. They are found in fruit.

▼ ① The five nutrient groups.

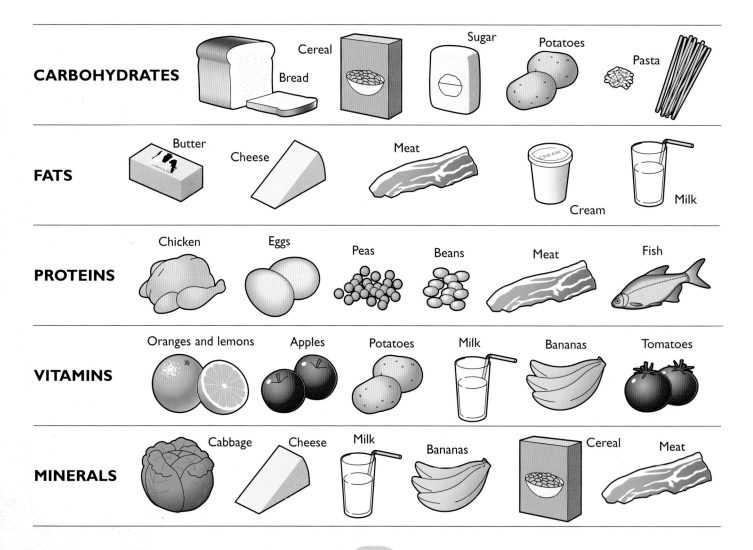

CARBOHYDRATES — Bread, Cereal, Sugar, Potatoes, Pasta

FATS — Butter, Cheese, Meat, Cream, Milk

PROTEINS — Chicken, Eggs, Peas, Beans, Meat, Fish

VITAMINS — Oranges and lemons, Apples, Potatoes, Milk, Bananas, Tomatoes

MINERALS — Cabbage, Cheese, Milk, Bananas, Cereal, Meat

Starches are made of long chains of particles that dissolve much more slowly. Starches are found in plant seeds (for example: wheat, rice, maize) and tubers (such as potatoes).

Using these two forms of energy, the body can get quick extra supplies of energy when it needs it, as well as a long term supply for normal uses.

Fat

The most concentrated form of energy is fat, a substance that makes up a large proportion of butter, cheese, milk and some kinds of meat and fish.

Fats are used as a reserve of energy. The body stores fat for use in emergencies. Most fat is stored just under the skin where it also helps to slow down heat loss.

Proteins

Proteins are used in making and repairing the body. The main foods which contain proteins are meat, fish, eggs, milk, peas, beans and cereals.

▲▶ ② Vitamins are important in controlling chemical reactions in the body. The body needs many vitamins. Only tiny amounts of vitamins are needed, but without them, the body cannot work properly. Each vitamin is found in a particular range of foods. For example, vitamin A is found in milk, butter and fish liver oils, while vitamin C is found in oranges, lemons, tomatoes and potatoes.

▶ ③ Minerals are chemicals which may be used to build the body or to help parts of the body work. The body needs a wide range of minerals. For example, the mineral calcium, found in milk and cheese, is used to make teeth and bones, and also to help blood clot after a cut. Many minerals are found in cereals, fruit and vegetables.

The mouth

Mouths are designed to do many jobs. Among the most important are breaking down food and tasting that it is fit to eat.

We use a combination of lips, teeth, **SALIVA** and tongue to check and break down food into the small pieces needed before we can swallow.

▼ ① **There are two sets of teeth, one in the roof of the mouth and one in the floor of the mouth.**

Teeth

There are 32 teeth in two rows around the front and sides of our mouths. Children have 28 teeth. The four 'wisdom teeth' only grow as we become adults. One row is in the roof of the mouth, the other is in the floor of the mouth (Pictures ① and ②). Their job is to tear and grind food. The roots of the teeth are covered in a soft tissue called the gums.

The incisor teeth at the front of our mouths are chisel-shaped to cut through our food. Behind them are the canine teeth, used for piercing and tearing. At the back of the mouth are broad, flat teeth called molars, used to crush food.

Lips hold food, prevent spillages and are sensitive to food that is too hot or too cold for our mouths.

The tongue is a large wedge-shaped muscle. We use it to move food around our mouth and to shape it for easy swallowing. **TASTE-BUDS** on the tongue check the chemicals in the food to make sure it is fit for eating.

Wisdom tooth

Molars

Canine

Incisors

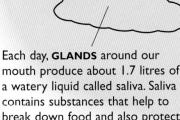

Each day, **GLANDS** around our mouth produce about 1.7 litres of a watery liquid called saliva. Saliva contains substances that help to break down food and also protect the mouth from **INFECTION.**

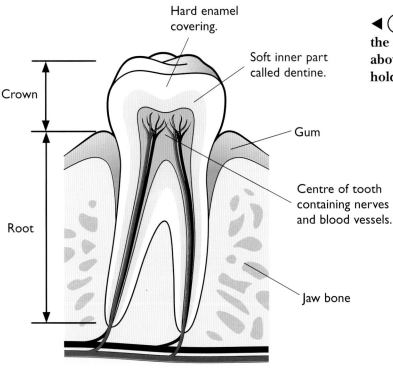

Hard enamel covering.

Soft inner part called dentine.

Crown

Root

Gum

Centre of tooth containing nerves and blood vessels.

Jaw bone

◀ ② There are two parts to a tooth: the crown (the white part you see above the gum) and the root, which holds the tooth in the gum.

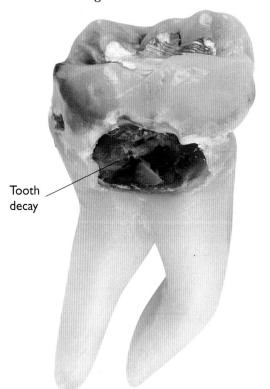

Tooth decay

▲ ③ The outer coating of the tooth is made of an especially hard material called enamel. It resists wear and acid attack.

The enamel protects a much softer part of the tooth which is made of a material called dentine. If the enamel wears away or acids destroy it, the dentine is easily removed, producing a cavity.

If the cavity gets large, the nerves in the centre of the tooth are exposed and then toothache begins.

Mouth care

The mouth is designed to be self-cleaning. However, some foods we eat allow a substance called **PLAQUE** to form on the crowns of the teeth.

Plaque is a mixture of saliva, food and **BACTERIA**. The bacteria feed on sugar in the food and as they do so they release **ACIDS**.

Bacteria can only become a problem if food is allowed to stay coating the teeth and gums. Regular brushing removes the plaque. Toothpaste also contains substances which counteract the acids, so they do not attack the teeth.

Foods that are made with sugar (like biscuits, sweets and soft drinks) cause the most problems. Foods that contain natural sugar (such as apples) do not encourage bacteria.

Tooth decay and gum problems

When acids form on the surface of teeth, they react chemically with the hard enamel coating and begin to dissolve it away. This is called tooth decay (Picture ③).

Bacteria can also invade the gums, attacking the roots and loosening the teeth.

13

Digestion

Digestion is the way food gets changed into substances the body can use. There are two stages of digestion: first the food is broken down and dissolved in liquids; then it is taken into the body.

Food is altered in the long, convoluted tube that leads from the mouth (Picture ①).

Vital stages
To give you some idea of what each part of the digestive system does, these pictures show a carrot treated to represent the way the system works and what the products look like.

▼ ① The digestive system.

Mouth
Teeth break down large lumps of food into smaller particles. The saliva begins the chemical process of breaking the food down.

Stomach
The food is churned over in the stomach and mixed with acid. This releases the different nutrients in the food and also kills germs.

Liver
The liver produces a digestive juice that helps break down fats.

Pancreas
The pancreas produces a digestive juice that breaks down proteins, fats and carbohydrates.

Small intestine
Here the food seeps through cell walls into the blood.

Large intestine
Here the water is extracted from the remains of the food and becomes urine. Solid wastes continue their journey in a compact, drier form.

Breaking food down

Because the body is really a chemical factory, chemical reactions work faster when they can work on small pieces of food. Chewing food turns large pieces into small fragments with a bigger surface area so the chemicals have more area to work on.

The body can only take in substances which dissolve in water, so to help the food we eat dissolve, the body produces chemicals, such as those in our saliva.

Where food is broken down

There is a short tube from the mouth to the stomach. There are muscles in the wall of the tube which make a kind of rippling motion, pushing the food down. You can feel this rippling motion when you swallow.

Acids that help break down proteins are added when the food reaches the bag called the stomach. The acids help to dissolve the food and also kill most harmful GERMS that might have been eaten.

Where the food is absorbed

Below the stomach is a long soft tube packed into the lower half of the body in zig-zag fashion. This is called the small INTESTINE. It is about seven metres long and its crinkly inside surface has a surface area as big as 17 tennis courts, some 4,500 square metres.

By now, nearly all of the nourishment from the food is dissolved in water, so it can seep through the walls of the small intestine and mix with the blood. In this way, nourishment is carried around the body to places where it is needed.

The remaining material is mostly FIBRE (Picture ②).

Removing the remains

Waste material such as fibre needs to be removed from the body. The rippling action takes the fibre through the large intestine, where water passes into the blood. At the bottom of the intestine the waste is ready to be expelled when we visit the toilet.

▶ ② How the small intestine digests food.

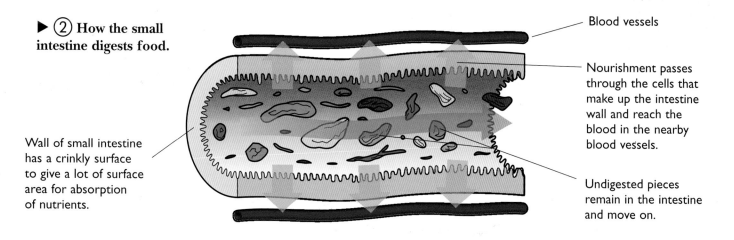

Wall of small intestine has a crinkly surface to give a lot of surface area for absorption of nutrients.

Blood vessels

Nourishment passes through the cells that make up the intestine wall and reach the blood in the nearby blood vessels.

Undigested pieces remain in the intestine and move on.

Weblink: www.CurriculumVisions.com/body

Breathing

A large part of the body is used for taking in oxygen and expelling waste gas. This process is called RESPIRATION.

Many of the chemical reactions that go on in the body use oxygen. All of the billions of cells in the body, for example, need oxygen.

As oxygen is used, a waste gas called carbon dioxide forms. This is what we breathe out. Breathing involves taking in new oxygen and expelling waste carbon dioxide.

Breathing

Every time we breathe in, we pull air containing oxygen into our lungs. To do this we need an air pump. But the lungs don't do the pumping. Instead, they act as a bellows bag which is squashed and stretched by muscles in the chest (Picture ①).

The air pathway

The nose and windpipe filter, moisten and warm the air as it is breathed in. Hairs in the nose filter out dust particles, and a sticky substance lining the walls of the nose traps bacteria.

The walls of the windpipe are lined with microscopic hairs. The hairs ripple upwards, pushing dirt and bacteria back up the windpipe.

In these ways bacteria and dirt are mainly kept out of the lungs.

Breathing out

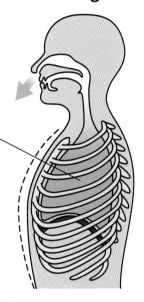

The muscles now relax and then automatically contract, letting the rib cage fall and the diaphragm rise. This makes the lungs smaller and pushes out stale air.

Breathing in

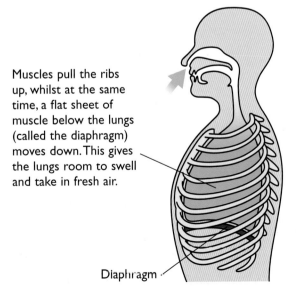

Muscles pull the ribs up, whilst at the same time, a flat sheet of muscle below the lungs (called the diaphragm) moves down. This gives the lungs room to swell and take in fresh air.

Diaphragm

◄▲ ① Breathing is controlled by muscles. Their job is to work the lungs as a kind of 'bellows'. They make the lungs pull in fresh air and push out stale air.

▼ ② **The parts of the body that help you to breathe.**

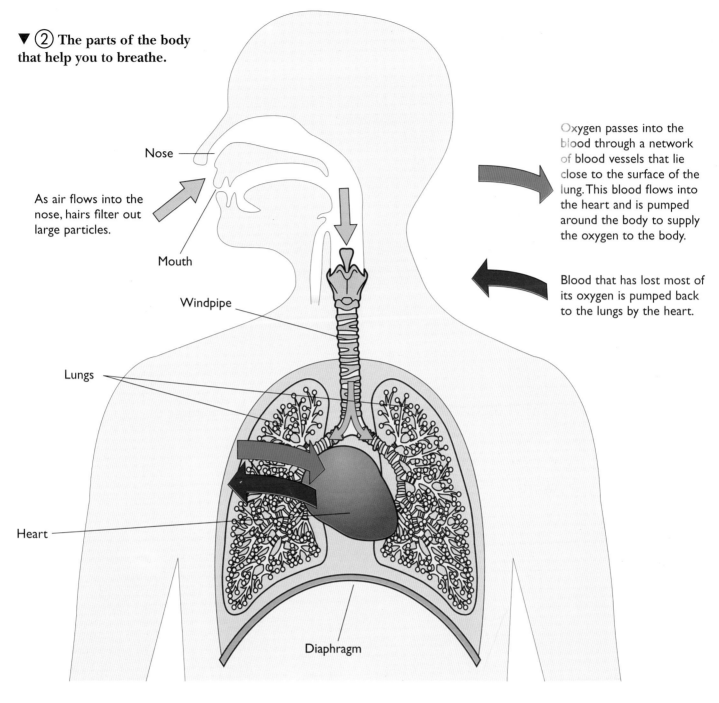

Nose

As air flows into the nose, hairs filter out large particles.

Mouth

Windpipe

Lungs

Heart

Diaphragm

Oxygen passes into the blood through a network of blood vessels that lie close to the surface of the lung. This blood flows into the heart and is pumped around the body to supply the oxygen to the body.

Blood that has lost most of its oxygen is pumped back to the lungs by the heart.

The lungs

There are two lungs in the chest (Picture ②). The job of the lungs is to allow the oxygen inside the lungs to move into the blood, which flows in a network of small blood vessels close to the lung surface.

Each lung has around 150 million tiny bubble-shaped lumps. They create a huge surface area of about 140 square metres.

At the same time as oxygen passes into blood, refreshing it, spent blood, containing carbon dioxide, reaches the lungs. The carbon dioxide seeps out into the lungs, just in time to be expelled as air is breathed out.

Weblink: www.CurriculumVisions.com/body

Blood

Blood looks like a red liquid, but it is really a mixture of solids in a liquid. It delivers nourishment, heat and oxygen to cells, and collects and removes waste.

The movement of blood around the body is called the circulation. It has three important purposes. It delivers oxygen and nourishment, takes away waste and carries heat (Picture ①).

The nature of blood

The blood is a mixture of solid particles carried along by a liquid. You can see this with a microscope.

A human body contains several litres of blood. The bigger the person, the more blood they have. Most adults, for example, have five or six litres of blood.

What the blood does

Nothing is actually made in the blood. Blood simply carries things made elsewhere to the parts of the body that need them.

You can compare blood to a river. First, think of a river seen from high in the air. You can see the route of the

▼ ① The tiny tubes carrying blood are called CAPILLARIES. They contain a liquid called plasma. Although it looks clear, it actually contains many substances in solution, just like water.

The plasma carries the blood cells, as well as other solid particles. The plasma is also like a central heating and cooling system, carrying heat to or from all parts of the body to keep a balanced temperature.

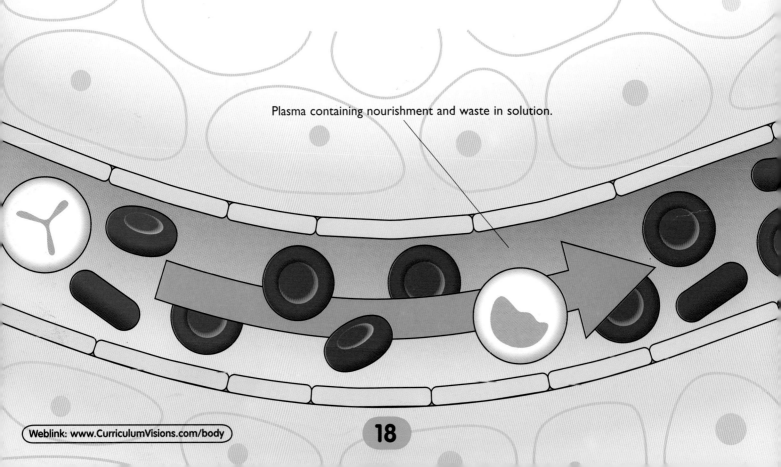

Plasma containing nourishment and waste in solution.

river, but you can't see the boulders, sand or clay carried in it. This is like looking at the blood if you cut yourself. It seems like a red liquid, because you are not looking closely enough to see the solid particles carried in it (Picture ②).

As soon as you look more closely you see the particles carried in the blood. You also see that some of the particles (the red blood cells) give the blood its red colour, while the liquid they are carried in is pale yellow. There are five million red blood cells in just one cubic millimetre drop of blood.

The blood also carries white blood cells that help the body to defend itself from disease or damage.

▼ ② A red blood cell is a tiny disc, just eight thousandths of a millimetre across.

Red blood cells contain an iron-rich substance called haemoglobin, which picks up oxygen from the lungs and gives blood its red colour.

A red blood cell has a life of about three months. Each second, over a million old red cells are replaced in the body by new cells made by the marrow inside the bones.

The picture below was taken through a powerful microscope so that you can see the red blood cells.

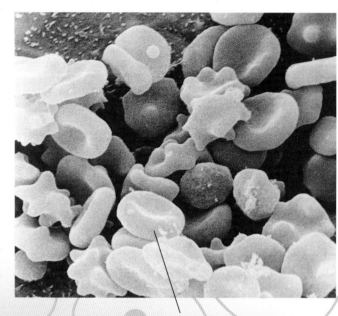

The particles shaped like discs in this picture are all red blood cells

Capillary wall is one cell thick.

Red blood cell

White blood cells to fight disease.

The heart

The heart is a pump made of muscle. Its job is to pump the blood around the body.

The circulation of the blood depends on the pumping action of the heart.

The heart lies in the front of the chest, a little to the left of centre (Picture ①). It is about the size of a clenched fist, but it is hollow inside. The heart is connected to the tubes (blood vessels) that carry blood around the body.

The heart

The walls of the heart are made from a thick, tough muscle that can relax and contract quickly every time it receives signals from the nerves.

The inside of the heart is divided into two halves by a muscle wall (Picture ②). Each side is itself divided horizontally by flaps of muscle called valves. As a result, the heart contains four chambers.

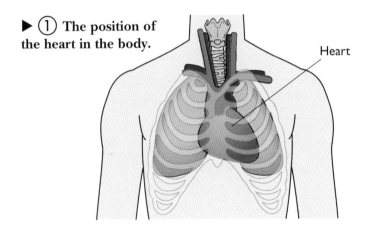

▶ ① **The position of the heart in the body.**

Heart

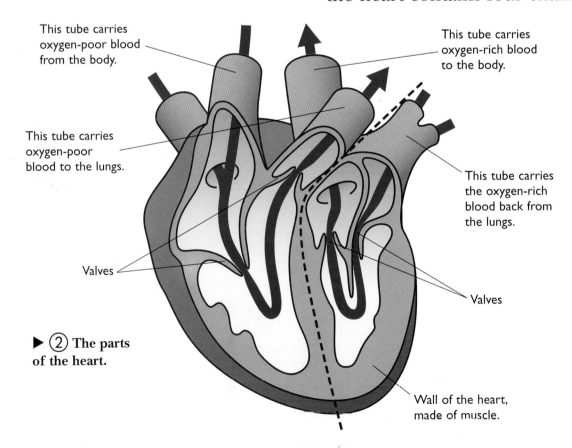

This tube carries oxygen-poor blood from the body.

This tube carries oxygen-poor blood to the lungs.

This tube carries oxygen-rich blood to the body.

This tube carries the oxygen-rich blood back from the lungs.

Valves

Valves

Wall of the heart, made of muscle.

▶ ② **The parts of the heart.**

The two chambers on the right of your heart receive oxygen-poor blood from the body and pump it through the lungs. The two chambers on the left receive blood from the lungs that is rich in oxygen and pump this around the body until it returns to the right side of the heart again (Picture ③).

The heart beat

When we listen to our heart beat it makes two separate noises that sound a bit like 'lub dup'. The stronger 'lub' sound is made when the valves between the chambers close. The weaker 'dup' sound is made when the valves forcing blood from the heart close. Taking a **PULSE** is another way to measure the heart beat.

▼ ③ How the heart pumps blood. The muscles in the walls of the chambers work together to pump the blood through the heart.

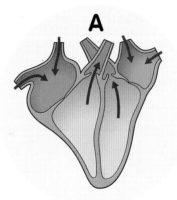

A

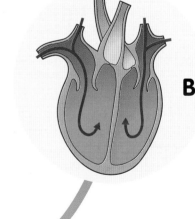

B

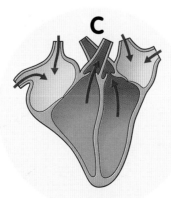

C

D

First, the muscles in the walls of the upper chambers relax and the blood from the veins flows into the upper part of the heart (stage **A**).

Next, when blood has filled the upper chambers, the muscles in the upper chamber walls squeeze together, pushing the blood through the valves to the lower chambers (stage **B**).

Then, these valves shut and the muscles in the lower chamber walls squeeze together; valves to the arteries then open, allowing blood to be pumped to the body (stage **C**).

These valves now close, preventing blood from flowing back into the heart (stage **D**).

The cycle now begins again.

Weblink: www.CurriculumVisions.com/body

How blood circulates

Blood circulates around the body through arteries and veins.

Blood circulates in two ways: around the body, and through the lungs. The heart is responsible for pumping blood around both systems.

Circulation to the body

When the blood leaves the heart it enters a plumbing system of tubes. The first tubes are wide. They are the arteries. Then the blood branches off into much smaller tubes called capillaries. Spent blood gets pushed from the capillaries into 'drains' – the veins – which take the blood back to the heart (Pictures ① and ②).

In this way, oxygen and nourishment from the blood can easily pass to the cells. At the same time, wastes such as carbon dioxide can pass from the cells back to the blood. As this happens, the blood changes colour from red to blue.

You can see some of these blue veins just below your skin.

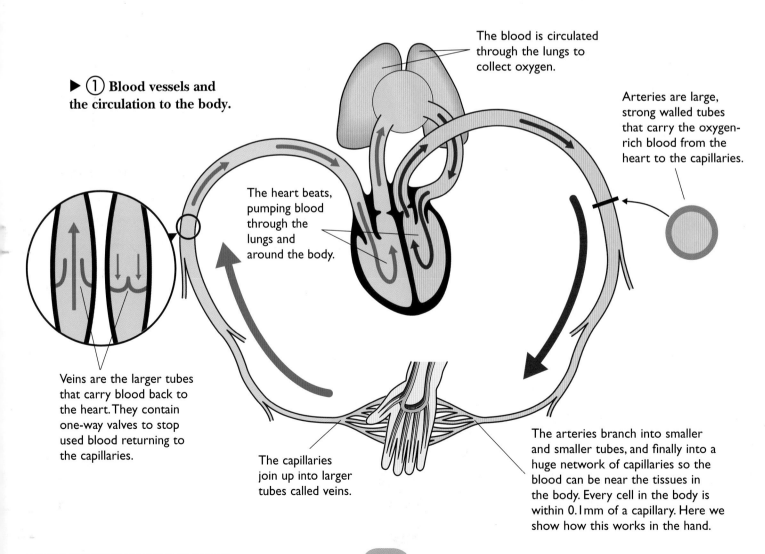

▶ ① **Blood vessels and the circulation to the body.**

The blood is circulated through the lungs to collect oxygen.

Arteries are large, strong walled tubes that carry the oxygen-rich blood from the heart to the capillaries.

The heart beats, pumping blood through the lungs and around the body.

Veins are the larger tubes that carry blood back to the heart. They contain one-way valves to stop used blood returning to the capillaries.

The capillaries join up into larger tubes called veins.

The arteries branch into smaller and smaller tubes, and finally into a huge network of capillaries so the blood can be near the tissues in the body. Every cell in the body is within 0.1mm of a capillary. Here we show how this works in the hand.

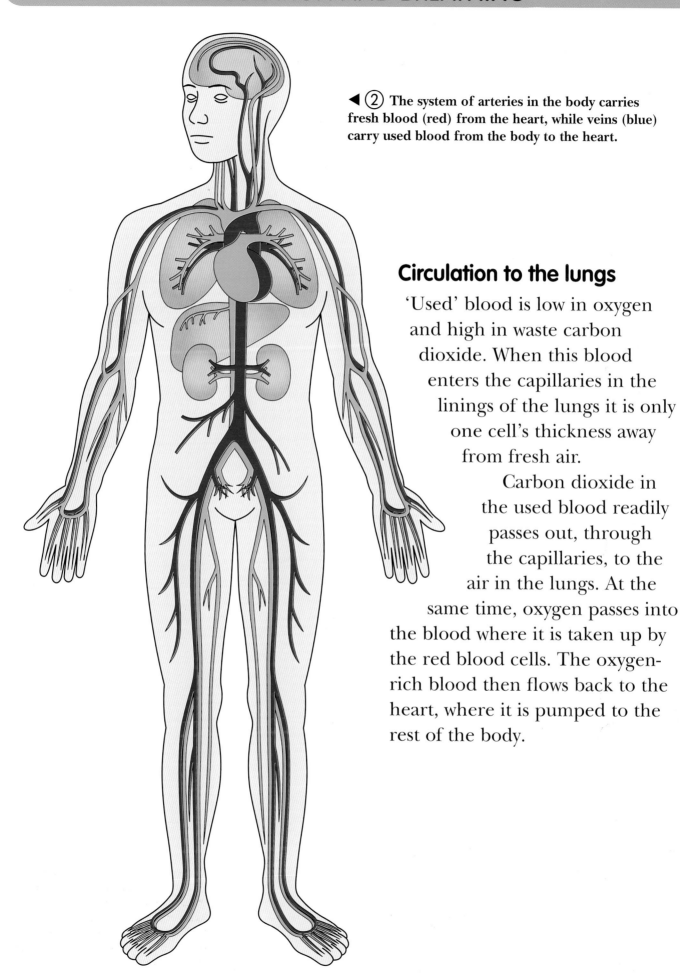

◀ ② The system of arteries in the body carries fresh blood (red) from the heart, while veins (blue) carry used blood from the body to the heart.

Circulation to the lungs

'Used' blood is low in oxygen and high in waste carbon dioxide. When this blood enters the capillaries in the linings of the lungs it is only one cell's thickness away from fresh air.

Carbon dioxide in the used blood readily passes out, through the capillaries, to the air in the lungs. At the same time, oxygen passes into the blood where it is taken up by the red blood cells. The oxygen-rich blood then flows back to the heart, where it is pumped to the rest of the body.

Weblink: www.CurriculumVisions.com/body

Bones

Bones give strength to the body, and also provide new cells for the blood.

Bones have different shapes and sizes to suit the jobs they have to perform (Picture ①). For example, bones that have to bear a great weight will be different in shape from those that have only a light weight to support.

Bones are not made of just one material. Many bones are made of a hard tube, inside which is soft, spongy bone containing a honeycomb of chambers filled with red **MARROW**.

▶ ① **The body contains four types of bones: long bones, short bones, flat bones and irregular bones.**

Flat bones
The shoulder blade is a flat bone. The skull and ribs also contain flat bones.

Long bones
These are the dumb-bell -shaped bones of the legs and arms. They consist of a long hollow shaft and two bulbous ends. The shaft needs to be strong and yet lightweight, so it is made of compact bone with a hollow core. The top end of this long bone forms the 'ball' in a ball and socket joint.

Irregular bones
Irregular bones occur where many bones fit together. The spine, the hands and the feet all contain irregular bones.

Short bones
These are found in places where many bones join, such as the fingers, wrists, ankles and toes.

The parts of a bone

All bones consist of many parts. In Picture ② you can see the parts of a long leg bone.

The main part of the bone is a strong tube made of thick compact bone. This kind of bone is as strong as iron, but a third of the weight.

At the very end of the bone is a layer of tissue called the **CARTILAGE**. This acts like a rubbery cushion and protects the bone from sudden jolts.

Bones are alive

At first sight, bones may seem to be just 'dead bone'. But they also contain living cells, as do all other parts of the body. These living cells allow the bones to grow or to mend. The centre of the bone contains marrow where blood cells are produced.

The shaft is filled with fatty yellow marrow in adults and with red marrow in growing children.

Hard bone

▶ ② **Inside a long bone.**

Each end of the bone is shaped to connect with other bones. The bone spreads out and is bulbous. This has two uses: the bulbous end gives a large surface area for the muscles to attach to; and it provides a large surface to form into a joint. A large bone joint is also stable and less likely to be pushed out of place.

The bone ends are made of spongy bone, whose honeycombed spaces are filled with red marrow.

The surface of the bone is covered with a white layer of fibres, a kind of 'skin'. This provides a good surface for muscles to attach to.

The 'skin' also contains tiny blood vessels and special cells that can help new bone to grow.

The surface blood vessels in the 'skin' send branches deep into the bone and supply bone cells with the oxygen and nourishment they need. They allow new blood cells to get from the marrow to the rest of the body.

Weblink: www.CurriculumVisions.com/body

The skeleton

The skeleton is made of 206 bones held together by muscles.

Bones make up the rigid framework that supports and protects the soft parts of the body. This is called the skeleton (Picture ①).

At the top is the skull – a set of curved plates that are wrapped around, and protect, the entire brain. Below it is the rib cage, which protects the lungs and heart.

People, like all large land animals, have an internal skeleton which grows with the rest of the body.

How a bone grows

When your skeleton first formed, the bones were soft. However, they soon began to change as well as grow. Soft bone became hard bone. Your bones will continue to grow in length until you are about eighteen years old.

Bones can regrow if they are broken (Picture ②), no matter what your age.

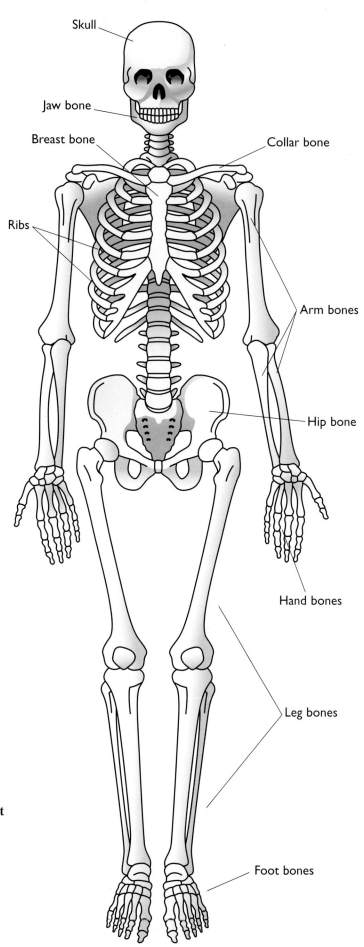

Skull

Jaw bone

Breast bone

Collar bone

Ribs

Arm bones

Hip bone

Hand bones

Leg bones

Foot bones

▶ ① Some of the important bones of the skeleton.

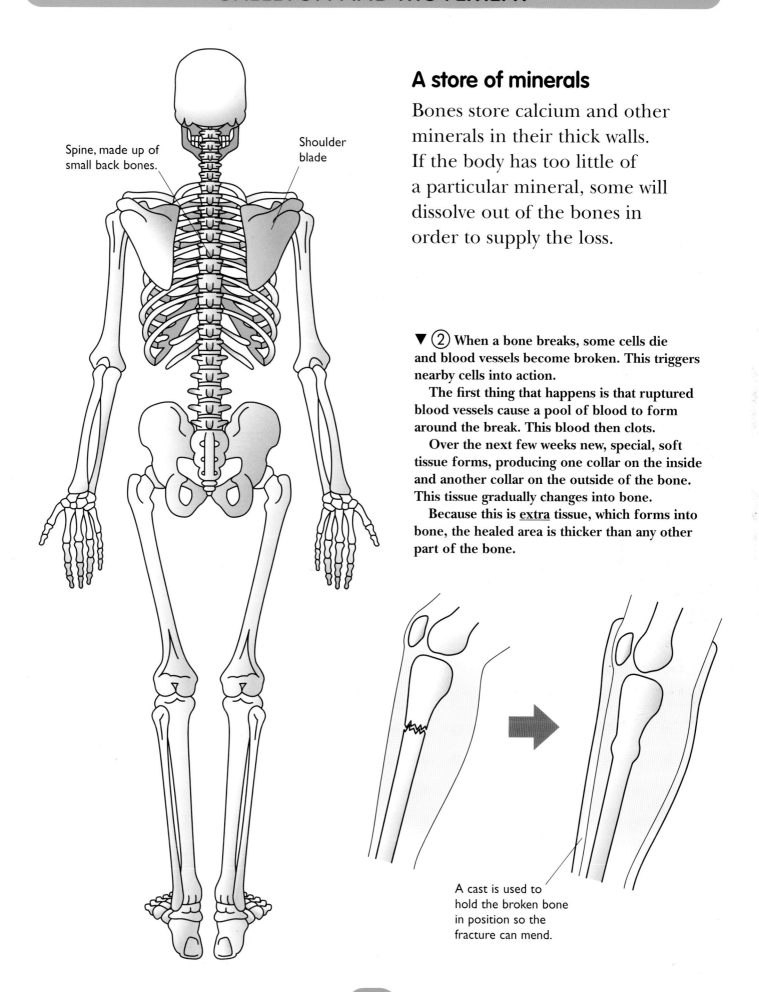

Spine, made up of small back bones.

Shoulder blade

A store of minerals

Bones store calcium and other minerals in their thick walls. If the body has too little of a particular mineral, some will dissolve out of the bones in order to supply the loss.

▼ ② When a bone breaks, some cells die and blood vessels become broken. This triggers nearby cells into action.

The first thing that happens is that ruptured blood vessels cause a pool of blood to form around the break. This blood then clots.

Over the next few weeks new, special, soft tissue forms, producing one collar on the inside and another collar on the outside of the bone. This tissue gradually changes into bone.

Because this is <u>extra</u> tissue, which forms into bone, the healed area is thicker than any other part of the bone.

A cast is used to hold the broken bone in position so the fracture can mend.

Weblink: www.CurriculumVisions.com/body

Joints

There are joints between nearly all bones. They allow the bones to move in a variety of ways.

The bones of the skull are fixed rigidly together. Most other bones in the body can move at their **JOINTS** (Picture ①).

Inside a joint

The ends of the bones are shaped to fit together closely with, for example, ridges and grooves, or balls and sockets (Pictures ② and ③). The shape of the end of the bone controls the range of movement that the joint can make.

▶▼ ① The main types of joints in the body.

Hinge joint
These joints allow easy movement in only two directions, such as up and down. Finger and toe joints are like this.

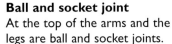

Ball and socket joint
At the top of the arms and the legs are ball and socket joints. These joints allow the limbs to be moved in every direction.

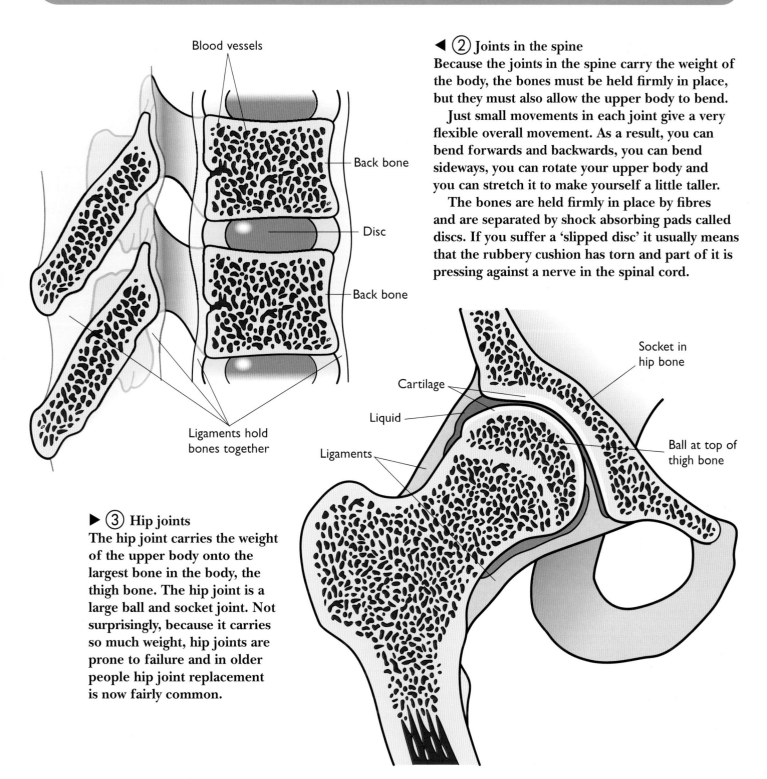

Blood vessels

Back bone

Disc

Back bone

Ligaments hold bones together

◄ ② Joints in the spine

Because the joints in the spine carry the weight of the body, the bones must be held firmly in place, but they must also allow the upper body to bend.

Just small movements in each joint give a very flexible overall movement. As a result, you can bend forwards and backwards, you can bend sideways, you can rotate your upper body and you can stretch it to make yourself a little taller.

The bones are held firmly in place by fibres and are separated by shock absorbing pads called discs. If you suffer a 'slipped disc' it usually means that the rubbery cushion has torn and part of it is pressing against a nerve in the spinal cord.

Socket in hip bone

Cartilage

Liquid

Ligaments

Ball at top of thigh bone

► ③ Hip joints

The hip joint carries the weight of the upper body onto the largest bone in the body, the thigh bone. The hip joint is a large ball and socket joint. Not surprisingly, because it carries so much weight, hip joints are prone to failure and in older people hip joint replacement is now fairly common.

Bones that have a lot of movement are held together by fibres called ligaments, and separated by cushioning pads (Picture ②). The pads contain a tough material with a slippery surface called cartilage.

It protects the ends of the bones from wear as they rub against each other during movement.

Joints where the bones can move contain a liquid which covers the cartilage. It acts like an oil to reduce wear on the cartilage surfaces.

Weblink: www.CurriculumVisions.com/body

Muscles

Bones cannot move on their own. They are moved by MUSCLES.

Our body contains over 600 muscles, making up about half our weight. Muscles help to shape the body, and they make up the bulk of the flesh that covers our bones (Picture ①).

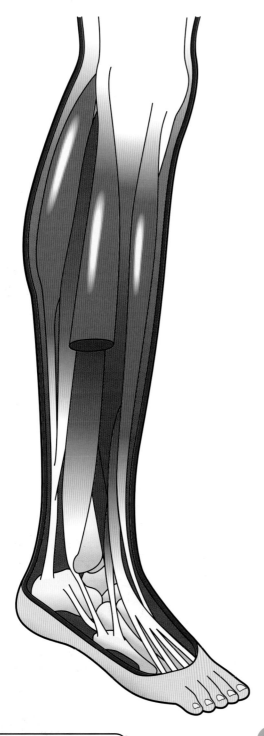

A muscle contains nerves and blood vessels. Each muscle is bound up in a very thin, tough, transparent bag of tissue that holds it all in place and separates it from other nearby muscles.

The nerves make sure that the brain can send messages to every part of the muscle. Blood flowing in the blood vessels provides oxygen and nourishment.

Muscles and joints

The joints contain no natural springs. All the movement at a joint is done by the muscles – even when we relax.

Muscles are normally found in pairs (Picture ②).

Heart muscle

The heart contains a special kind of muscle. We have no control of our heart muscle. The rhythm of beating is set by an internal pacemaker. All the brain can do is to send signals that speed up or slow down the rate of beating.

◀ ① Muscles in the lower leg. Notice how they wrap around the bone and across the ankle and foot joints.

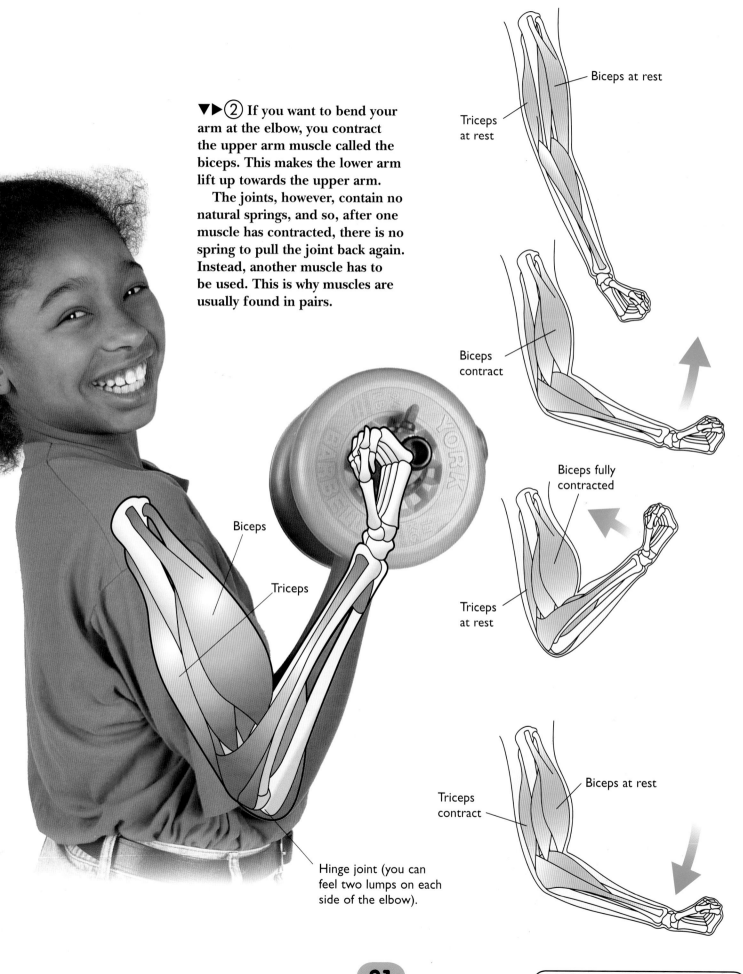

▼▶② If you want to bend your arm at the elbow, you contract the upper arm muscle called the biceps. This makes the lower arm lift up towards the upper arm.

The joints, however, contain no natural springs, and so, after one muscle has contracted, there is no spring to pull the joint back again. Instead, another muscle has to be used. This is why muscles are usually found in pairs.

Biceps at rest

Triceps at rest

Biceps contract

Biceps fully contracted

Triceps at rest

Triceps contract

Biceps at rest

Biceps

Triceps

Hinge joint (you can feel two lumps on each side of the elbow).

The brain

The nervous system, including the brain, controls how the body works.

The body cannot work without receiving instructions. The instructions are handled by the brain (Picture ①).

The brain needs to receive information before it can send out the correct instructions. To do this there is a network of special cells, called nerves, that connect every part of the body to the brain (Picture ②).

Getting the information

Information is gathered and passed to the nerves, by special, sensitive cells. They occur all over the skin, inside the body, at the ears, eyes and so on. Information about past events is stored in special parts of the brain. We call this memory.

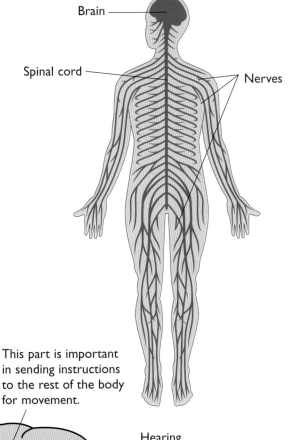

▼ ② How the brain is connected to the nerves.

Brain

Spinal cord

Nerves

This part is important in sending instructions to the rest of the body for movement.

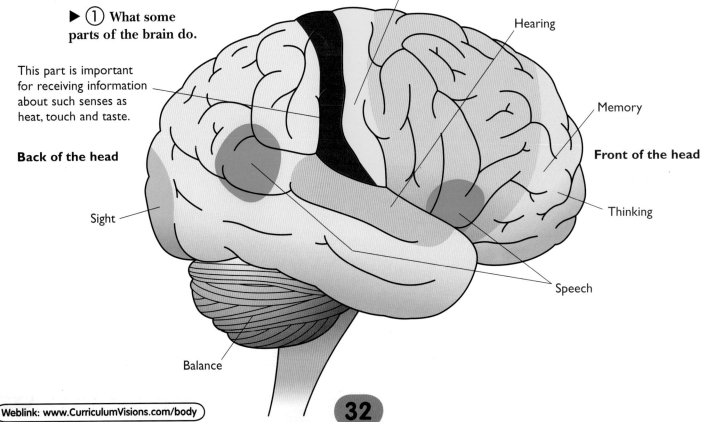

► ① What some parts of the brain do.

This part is important for receiving information about such senses as heat, touch and taste.

Back of the head

Sight

Balance

Hearing

Memory

Front of the head

Thinking

Speech

Whenever a nerve receives information, it causes a chemical reaction to occur and this, in turn, sets off electrical signals. The signals move almost instantly to the brain.

The brain then sends new instructions to whichever part of the body needs them. For example, information from the ears or eyes may cause the brain to send signals to nerves in the muscles of the arm, which cause the arm to move (Picture ③).

▼ ③ The 'simple' task of having a drink.

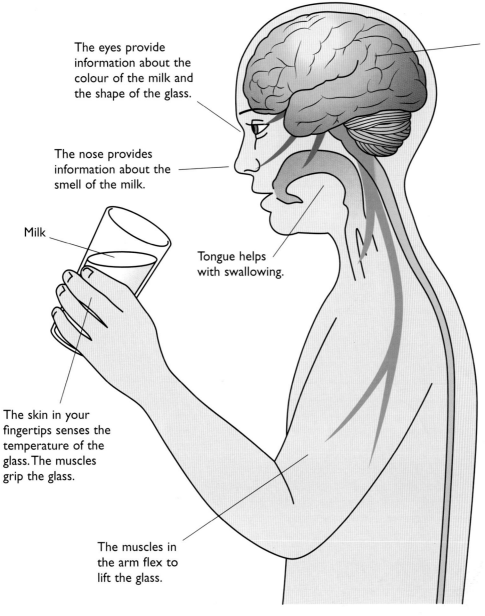

The eyes provide information about the colour of the milk and the shape of the glass.

The nose provides information about the smell of the milk.

Milk

Tongue helps with swallowing.

The skin in your fingertips senses the temperature of the glass. The muscles grip the glass.

The muscles in the arm flex to lift the glass.

The brain processes the information provided and immediately gives a complicated set of instructions. As a result, you instantly judge whether you like the smell and colour of the drink, what way the glass should be held and how it should be placed against your mouth.

Although you rely on the eyes to guide the glass to your mouth, the lips are used to hold it against the mouth. Meanwhile, the brain will be instructing glands in your mouth to produce saliva, and your throat to swallow the milk.

Weblink: www.CurriculumVisions.com/body

A new human life begins

Human life depends on passing on chemical instructions to new cells.

For any new human life to begin, it needs the right set of ingredients to make new cells, and some instructions for how to make them (Picture ①). The instructions are chemical packages called **GENES** (Picture ②). They contain the information for making all other chemicals needed for life.

Genes

Think of the way genes work as a recipe book which lays down rules for mixing the ingredients.

There are more than 60 billion cells in the human body and nearly all of them have their own genetic information. Each cell holds the instructions for how we develop.

Fertilisation

Men carry half of the instructions to form new life in special cells called **SPERM**, and women the other half in special cells called **EGGS**.

A man and a woman have to have to unite to provide a way for the sperm to reach the eggs (Picture ③).

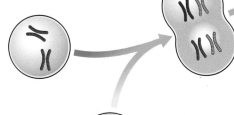

▼ ① When the sperm and egg cells combine, material from both cells mixes together to allow a new life to form.

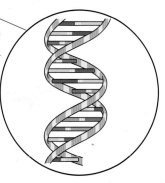

▶ ② A gene is a specific piece of information in the form of a chemical instruction.

Very large numbers of such genes are needed to provide the recipe for a living thing. They are found on threads called CHROMOSOMES inside the middle part of the cell, called the nucleus.

▼ ③ The sperm has to travel to the egg. This is easier if it is carrying relatively little 'baggage'. So it is 'slimmed down', mainly containing just chromosomes. It grows a tail to help it swim to the egg.

The female egg does not travel and so it keeps most of the original cell material and is larger, containing not just chromosomes, but other essential materials for making new cells.

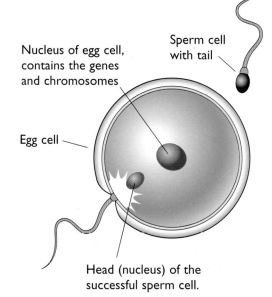

Nucleus of egg cell, contains the genes and chromosomes

Sperm cell with tail

Egg cell

Head (nucleus) of the successful sperm cell.

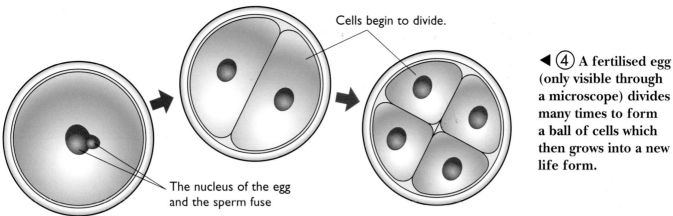

Cells begin to divide.

The nucleus of the egg and the sperm fuse

◀ ④ A fertilised egg (only visible through a microscope) divides many times to form a ball of cells which then grows into a new life form.

▼ ⑤ The early stages of life inside the womb.

During **FERTILISATION**, the genes from each parent combine to form a complete set of instructions again. The newly fertilised egg can now begin to grow.

Growing

The fertilised egg grows by dividing many many times (Picture ④).

During the earliest stages of growth the new life does not look much like a human. But as cells are instructed to specialise in various ways, so it becomes a much more recognisable shape.

Human life begins as a tiny, shapeless ball of cells which become tissue which then folds, changes shape and grows to form limbs (Picture ⑤). During this process genes instruct cells how to give the properties that will provide for life.

Once a baby is born the changes do not, of course, stop, but continue throughout life. But by birth, the fastest changes are finished and, as people get older, the changes occur more and more slowly.

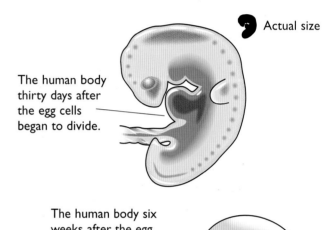

Actual size

The human body thirty days after the egg cells began to divide.

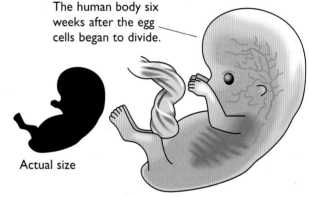

The human body six weeks after the egg cells began to divide.

Actual size

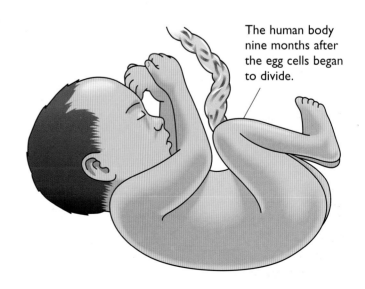

The human body nine months after the egg cells began to divide.

Weblink: www.CurriculumVisions.com/body

Bacteria and viruses

Bacteria and viruses are two kinds of tiny organisms that attack the body and cause disease.

The body is open to attack by all kinds of unseen microscopic bodies. These include **BACTERIA** and **VIRUSES**.

Bacteria are true living things. They form tiny capsules, called spores, which allow them to pass from one body to another without being killed by heat or by drying out.

Viruses do not appear to be alive, and so the body does not think it has to defend itself against them.

Bacterial spores and viruses may enter the body from the air, or in droplets of moisture from a sneeze or a cough. They may also enter in food and water or through a cut in the skin.

▼ ① **How a virus infects cells in the body.**

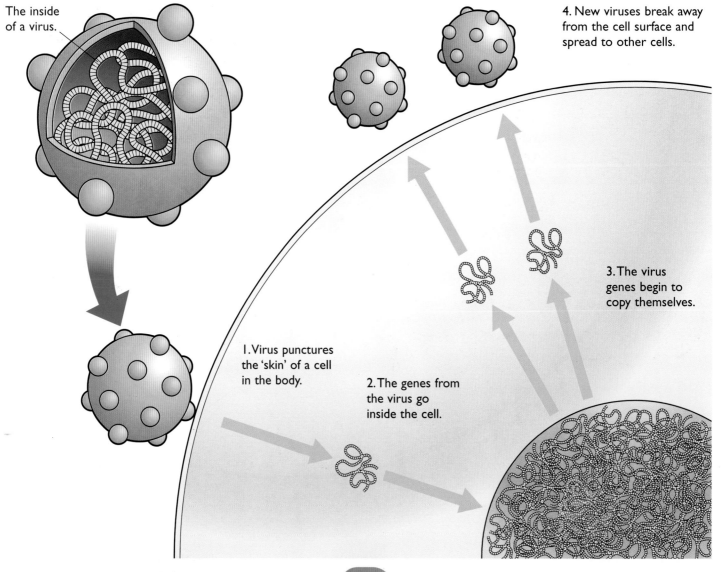

The inside of a virus.

4. New viruses break away from the cell surface and spread to other cells.

1. Virus punctures the 'skin' of a cell in the body.

2. The genes from the virus go inside the cell.

3. The virus genes begin to copy themselves.

How bacteria and viruses breed

When bacterial spores reach the moist, warm conditions inside the body, they break open and the bacteria inside them begin to spread out.

A virus needs to enter a cell to breed. It uses material inside the cell to make many offspring. This kills the cell. The offspring leave the dead cell and enter other living cells so they can also breed (Picture ①).

How diseases develop

The body does not react to infection immediately. For a while, the bacteria or viruses breed and produce poisons which destroy cells. It is only when their numbers become very large that the disease becomes obvious.

How germs are destroyed

Once a disease is inside the bloodstream, the body has an army of self-defence agents. Chief among these are white blood cells (Picture ②). One cubic millimetre of blood contains around 12,000 white blood cells (Picture ③). These destroy harmful bacteria and viruses.

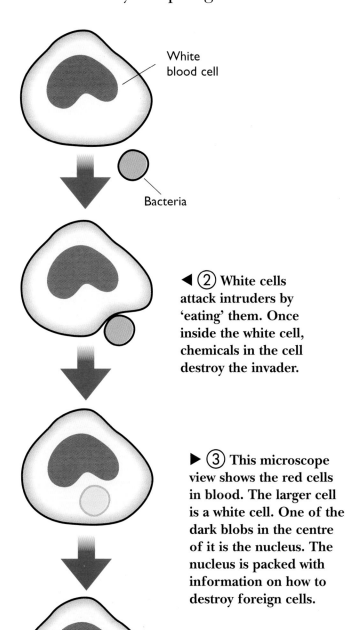

White blood cell

Bacteria

◀ ② **White cells attack intruders by 'eating' them. Once inside the white cell, chemicals in the cell destroy the invader.**

▶ ③ **This microscope view shows the red cells in blood. The larger cell is a white cell. One of the dark blobs in the centre of it is the nucleus. The nucleus is packed with information on how to destroy foreign cells.**

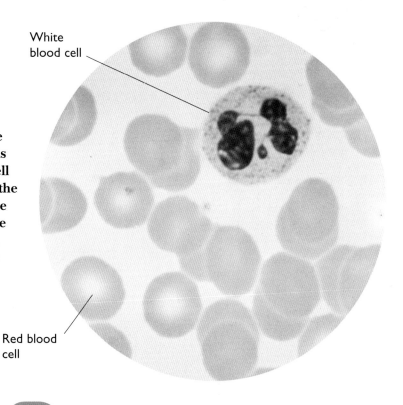

White blood cell

Red blood cell

Weblink: www.CurriculumVisions.com/body

Getting immunity

The body has a defence system to destroy harmful germs. Scientists have found ways to give our defence system extra help in fighting disease.

Many diseases can be passed from one person to another. The diseases produced by bacteria and viruses are infections of this kind.

The body's defences – called the **IMMUNE SYSTEM** – protects against infectious disease, but it may also sometimes cause disease.

Allergies

The immune system may react to any foreign substance, and it may mistake a perfectly harmless substance for an infection. This unfortunate effect is called an **ALLERGY**.

▲ ① **Antiseptics are usually cream or liquids that are applied directly to cuts.**

Medicines

Medicines are chemicals which destroy germs. Common medicines include antiseptics (Picture ①) and antibiotics (Picture ②).

An antibiotic is a substance which kills bacteria within the body. Penicillin was one of the first antibiotics discovered. It is made from a fungus.

An antiseptic is a chemical that is applied to a cut in the skin, where it kills any bacteria that are present. Antiseptics are often made in the form of ointments.

Disinfectants are antiseptic chemicals used

▶ ② **How the immune system and antibiotics deal with bacteria.**

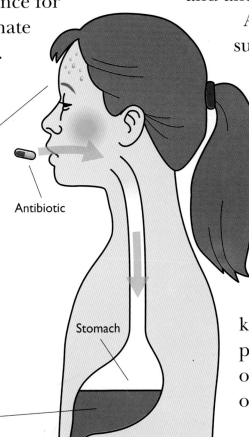

In this case bacteria have entered the digestive system and caused a stomach upset. The body's immune system tries to destroy the bacteria. The conflict between the body and the invading bacteria causes a reaction and if severe we experience an extreme reaction such as a fever or stomach pains. In such circumstances a doctor may advise that you take antibiotics.

Antibiotics can help the body's immune system by killing some of the harmful bacteria – making it easier for the body to destroy the rest.

Antibiotic

Stomach

to kill germs in the home. Many of these are too strong to use on skin. For example bleach is a strong disinfectant that kills germs in the home but it irritates the skin.

Vaccines and viruses

It takes time for the body's immune system to 'learn' how to destroy a new germ. As a result, sometimes when a body becomes infected with a germ, the germ can breed faster than the body is able to defend itself.

However, if the body has previously been subjected to small amounts of the germ, then it will have had time to build up defences against it (Picture ③). A **VACCINE** is a mixture of either weakened or killed germs, or the poisons produced by the germs. These cause the body to produce defences which remain ready to fight a future infection. Protection of this kind is called **IMMUNITY**. Vaccines are given either by injection or by mouth.

Vaccines can be made from both bacteria or viruses, although so far they have worked best against viruses. Common vaccines include those to protect against measles, hepatitis, polio, diphtheria, whooping cough, smallpox, rabies, typhoid, tuberculosis, tetanus, cholera and yellow fever.

So far, no one has developed a vaccine for the viruses that cause the common cold.

▼ ③ **How vaccines work against viruses.**

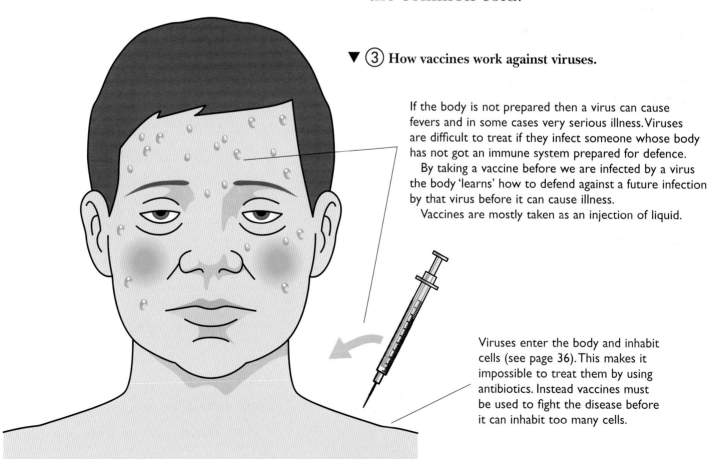

If the body is not prepared then a virus can cause fevers and in some cases very serious illness. Viruses are difficult to treat if they infect someone whose body has not got an immune system prepared for defence.

By taking a vaccine before we are infected by a virus the body 'learns' how to defend against a future infection by that virus before it can cause illness.

Vaccines are mostly taken as an injection of liquid.

Viruses enter the body and inhabit cells (see page 36). This makes it impossible to treat them by using antibiotics. Instead vaccines must be used to fight the disease before it can inhabit too many cells.

A healthy diet

Your body needs a certain amount of nourishment and energy if it is to stay healthy. How much you need depends on what you are doing.

The food that you eat over a period of time such as a day, week or year is called your **DIET**.

The body gets its nourishment and energy from food. Clearly, the body will only be healthy if it gets the right amount of both of these (Picture ①). This is called a balanced diet (Picture ②). But how do we know what 'enough' means, and how can we tell if our diet is balanced?

▼ ① Drinks often provide energy and nourishment, just as food does.

Weight

First, it helps to know that the body is very good at looking after itself. It also helps to know that the body likes to have plenty of insurance, so if it can store food in case of emergencies, it will. The difficulty is that the more it stores, the heavier the body becomes and the harder some other parts of the body have to work.

So a healthy diet for fully grown people is, in part, one where the body does not gain or lose weight. On the other hand, younger people are growing and so getting heavier all the time. In this case, getting heavier may be normal, but getting lighter is not.

Daily needs

A simple rule for eating a balanced diet is to eat one portion of meat and one portion of dairy products a day, and one or more portions of each of the other groups, such as fruit, shown in the picture opposite (Picture ③).

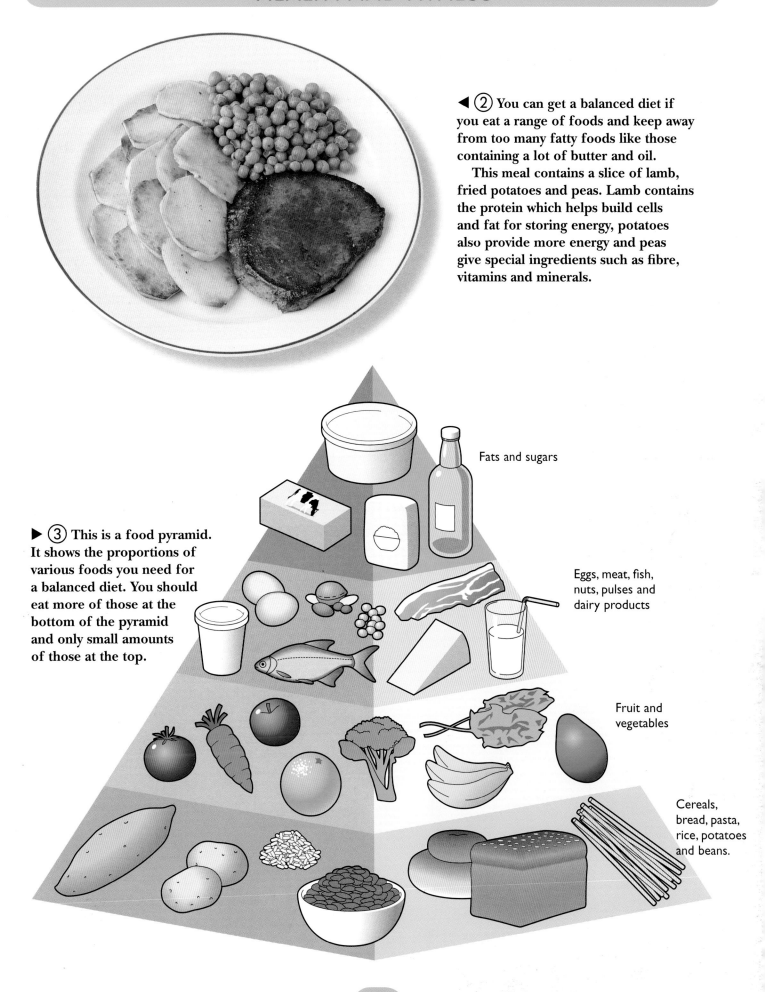

◄ ② You can get a balanced diet if you eat a range of foods and keep away from too many fatty foods like those containing a lot of butter and oil.

This meal contains a slice of lamb, fried potatoes and peas. Lamb contains the protein which helps build cells and fat for storing energy, potatoes also provide more energy and peas give special ingredients such as fibre, vitamins and minerals.

► ③ This is a food pyramid. It shows the proportions of various foods you need for a balanced diet. You should eat more of those at the bottom of the pyramid and only small amounts of those at the top.

Fats and sugars

Eggs, meat, fish, nuts, pulses and dairy products

Fruit and vegetables

Cereals, bread, pasta, rice, potatoes and beans.

Weblink: www.CurriculumVisions.com/body

Keeping fit

The body only works well if it gets enough exercise and has the right balance of foods. This is why.

When you exercise, you improve the health of heart, lungs, muscles, joints and bones.

Muscles

When muscles are not used, the body thinks it doesn't need to spend effort on keeping muscles strong because they are not asked to do much. As a result, the muscles get smaller and weaker (Picture ①). Then, when you do need to do something strenuous, you can't, because your muscles are too weak.

Exercise prevents muscles from wasting away. While you are growing, exercise also helps the bones to form properly.

Heart

Like all muscles, the heart also becomes stronger and works better if it is regularly exercised.

A strong heart pumps more blood with each beat, and so does not need to beat as fast to provide all the parts of the body with the food and oxygen it needs.

▼ ① **(A)** A leg-injury such as a broken bone. **(B)** The leg has to be put in plaster and cannot move. Muscle wasting occurs. **(C)** The plaster is removed, but the leg needs the support of crutches until the leg muscles are restored **(D)**.

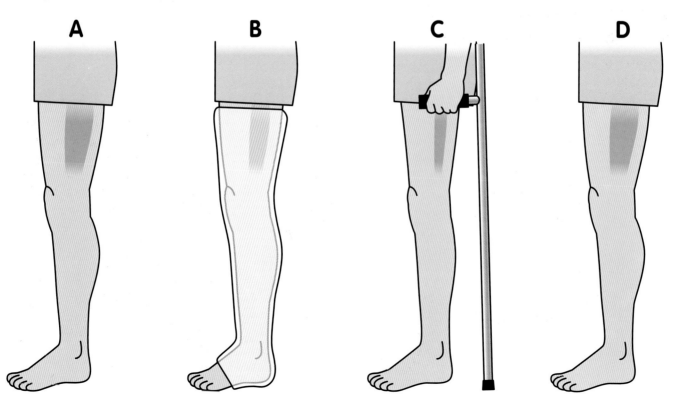

A　　　　　B　　　　　C　　　　　D

▼ ② **How fat builds up on artery walls.**

Blood flows normally through artery.

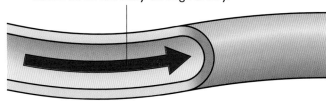

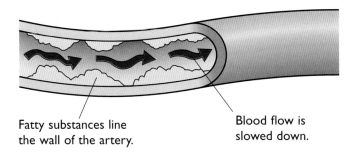

Fatty substances line the wall of the artery.

Blood flow is slowed down.

If the heart is strong, when you need to exert yourself, it can cope without having to beat too fast. A heart which has to beat fast is in danger of being overworked.

Arteries

The main tubes carrying the blood around the body are the arteries. Fatty substances from food can form a coating inside arteries so there is less room for the blood to flow (Picture ②). This is the main form of heart disease.

The heart has to push with greater force (called high blood pressure) when the arteries are narrowed.

In some cases, the fatty coating may break up and pieces may block the arteries, stopping the flow of blood. The result may be a heart attack.

Heart disease can be prevented by exercise and by eating a balanced diet.

Lungs

Any type of dust or foreign particles can settle in the lungs. This clogs their surfaces and causes irritation. This is especially true of the bottom of the lungs.

When people are at rest, oxygen only circulates in the top part of the lungs. The lower parts of the lungs are used when more oxygen is needed, such as when we exercise (Picture ③). So exercise helps to clear out the lungs.

◄ ③ **Exercise like running helps the lungs stay healthy, by forcing us to use the lower parts of the lungs.**

Weblink: www.CurriculumVisions.com/body

Taking risks

We can sometimes choose to override the body's defences. Doing this occasionally may cause little damage, but doing it often can cause permanent harm.

The body is a very tolerant chemistry set. But there are limits to what it can take, and when these limits are exceeded then things may start to go wrong. So if we choose to go outside the limits, then we are taking risks with our bodies.

The effects of smoking

Some chemicals, such as those in tobacco smoke, affect our breathing. For example, the chemicals can block the lungs from absorbing oxygen or they may stop dirt in the throat from

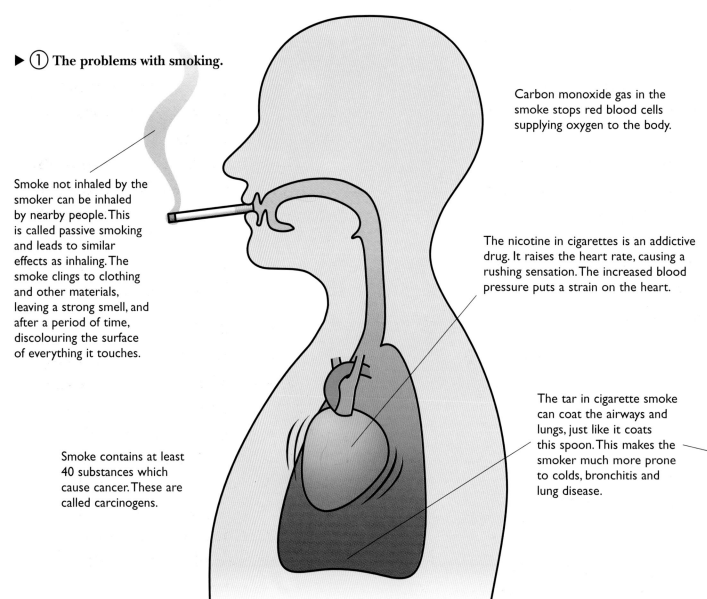

▶ ① **The problems with smoking.**

Smoke not inhaled by the smoker can be inhaled by nearby people. This is called passive smoking and leads to similar effects as inhaling. The smoke clings to clothing and other materials, leaving a strong smell, and after a period of time, discolouring the surface of everything it touches.

Smoke contains at least 40 substances which cause cancer. These are called carcinogens.

Carbon monoxide gas in the smoke stops red blood cells supplying oxygen to the body.

The nicotine in cigarettes is an addictive drug. It raises the heart rate, causing a rushing sensation. The increased blood pressure puts a strain on the heart.

The tar in cigarette smoke can coat the airways and lungs, just like it coats this spoon. This makes the smoker much more prone to colds, bronchitis and lung disease.

▼ ② **Substance abuse is often addictive (habit-forming). Addicts stop taking care of themselves, so they exercise little, eat poorly and become prone to disease.**

Drugs such as LSD (Acid), heroin and cocaine can cause severe brain damage.

Chemicals such as solvents cause severe damage to the lungs and brain.

Drugs can alter the state of mind, making the user see things that do not exist, become unnaturally active, have dulled senses or even become violent. People's reactions to drugs vary and are unpredictable.

Alcohol is also an addictive drug and can destroy the liver and other organs.

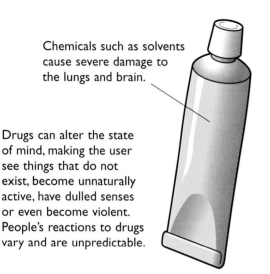
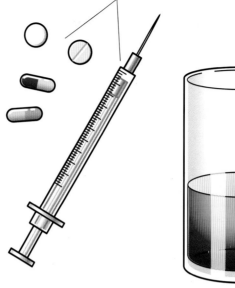

being removed naturally. As a result, bacteria and viruses can reach the lungs (Picture ①).

If germs get to the lungs, the only way the body can destroy them is by using white cells in the blood. This causes an irritation to the airways called bronchitis. The body then attempts to clear the lungs by coughing.

Coughing is a very violent activity, and if it is repeated over a long time it can damage lung tissue.

The chemicals in smoke may also affect the way some of the cells grow and make them develop abnormally. This is called cancer. In time, the cancer cells may spread through the body and may cause death.

Substance abuse

Alcohol and the chemicals in many solvents and some drugs affect the way the brain cells work. If alcohol is drunk in large amounts, solvents, like glue, are sniffed, or certain drugs are taken, a person's behaviour changes. If they are taken in very large quantities they can destroy brain cells or kill (Picture ②).

Weblink: www.CurriculumVisions.com/body

Glossary

ABSORB To soak up.

ACID A liquid which can eat away at other materials. Also, another word for the drug LSD.

ALLERGY A condition in which the immune system of the body reacts to a harmless substance as if the substance was harmful.

BACTERIA Tiny organisms which feed by digesting things around them such as sugar in the mouth. Some feed inside the body and make poisons which cause disease. The single of bacteria is bacterium.

BOWEL The lowest part of the intestine.

CAPILLARY A very narrow blood vessel just wide enough to let rows of red blood cells pass along it. It connects arteries to veins.

CARBOHYDRATES The foods starch, sugar and fibre. Starch and sugar provide energy while fibre helps the food move along the intestines.

CARTILAGE A tough, slippery, rubbery material on the ends of bones.

CELLS Tiny pieces of the body less than a tenth of a millimetre across. A cell is composed of a thin skin called a membrane, and contains a jelly like substance and a speck of darker material called a nucleus.

CHOLESTEROL Fatty substances that occur naturally in the blood, but which can, if present in large amounts, become stuck to the sides of the arteries and slow down the flow of blood to the heart.

CHROMOSOME A thread containing the genes which appears in a cell nucleus before the cell divides.

CIRCULATION The movement of blood through the heart, arteries, capillaries and veins.

DIET The range of foods that a person normally eats (going on a diet, on the other hand, commonly means to eat a special range of foods in order to lose weight).

DIGEST A process in which the body makes food particles so small that they can dissolve in water and pass through the wall of the small intestine into the blood.

DISEASE A condition that causes someone to be ill.

DISSOLVE A process in which a substance breaks up into such small particles when it enters a liquid that it cannot be seen.

EGG The sex cell produced by the female. A baby gets half of its genes from its mother from the nucleus in the egg.

ENERGY The ability to do work or make something change. The energy we need for our bodies comes from the complicated chemical reactions that take place as we digest the food and liquids we eat and drink.

FAT Food substances which store energy. However, if the body receives too much fat health may suffer.

FERTILISED, FERTILISATION The process in which the nucleus of the sperm joins with the nucleus of the egg and makes a fertilised egg.

FIBRE A carbohydrate which cannot be digested by the body but helps food move through the intestines.

GENE A structure in a cell nucleus which contains a piece of information to make the body develop in a certain way such as to grow brown hair or develop blue eyes.

GERM A small mass of living material capable of developing into an organism that might cause disease.

GLAND A group of cells which make a liquid that they release into the body. Lymph glands make white blood cells which fight disease.

GUT The tube which runs through the body from the mouth to the anus which is concerned with the digestion of food. Most of the gut is made of the small intestine.

IMMUNE, IMMUNE SYSTEM, IMMUNITY A system of glands and the marrow in some bones which produce white cells to fight disease. Immunity is a condition of the body in which it is protected from a disease.

INFECTION The invasion of the body by any germs including bacteria and viruses and the way the body reacts to them or to the poisons they make.

INTESTINE The long tube that leads from the stomach. It is mostly comprised of the small intestine which is the region of the digestive system where food is absorbed into the body.

JOINT A place in the skeleton where bones fit together.

MARROW A tissue in bones which makes blood cells.

MINERALS Food substances which are made from just one chemical such as calcium or iron. Minerals perform important tasks in keeping the body healthy.

MUSCLE The flesh in our body that can contract or relax to move our bones and our heart.

NERVES Cells which transmit electrical signals between different parts of the body. Nerve fibre is the long branch of a nerve cell which transmits electrical signals through the body.

NOURISHMENT Another way of saying food. A nutrient is a substance which is needed in the nourishment of the body such as protein or a vitamin or mineral.

NUCLEUS The centre of a cell. It contains the material that gives instructions as to how the cell will develop.

ORGANISM A word for any living thing. Usually applied to very small living things.

PLAQUE A coating on the crowns of teeth which may lead to tooth decay.

PROTEIN A food substance which is found particularly in meat and peas and beans and is used for the growth and repair of the body.

PULSE The throbbing of the artery which can be felt in the wrist or the neck which is caused by the heart beat.

REPRODUCTION The making of a new individual.

RESPIRATION Another term for breathing.

SALIVA The watery liquid which is made in structures called salivary glands under the tongue and in the cheeks. It makes the food easier to swallow and contains a chemical which digests starch to sugar.

SPERM The sex cell produced by the male. A baby gets half of its genes from its father from the nucleus in the sperm.

STARCH A form of carbohydrate that releases energy slowly. It is found in cereals.

TASTE-BUDS Groups of nerve cells in the tongue which are sensitive to chemicals in our food which make it sweet, salty, sour or bitter.

VACCINE A liquid which protects the body from a disease.

VIRUS A minute structure which behaves as though it were not alive when outside the body but can reproduce in cells and cause disease.

VITAMINS Food substances which are made from many different chemicals. They perform many important tasks in keeping the body healthy.

Index